Let's find out about . . .
RECYCLING

Dr. Mike Goldsmith

Tick Tock Books

Studio Manager: Sara Greasley
Editor: Belinda Weber
Designer: Trudi Webb
Production Controller: Ed Green
Production Manager: Suzy Kelly

ISBN: 978-1-84898-088-4
Tracking number: 3374LPP1209

Copyright © *TickTock* Entertainment Ltd. 2010
This edition produced for Scholastic Inc. 2010
First published in Great Britain in 2010 by *TickTock* Entertainment Ltd.,
The Old Sawmill, 103 Goods Station Road, Tunbridge Wells, Kent TN1 2DP, U.K.

Printed in China
9 8 7 6 5 4 3 2 1

Picture credits (t=top; b=bottom; c=center; l=left; r=right; OFC=outside front cover; OBC=outside back cover):
Action Press/Rex Features: 16b. Scott R. Barbour/Getty Images: 23b. bilderlounge/Getty Images: 4l. Photo
provided by the City & County of Honolulu: 15cl. Andy Drysdale/Rex Features: 22–23t. HotRot: 20–21c. iStock:
OFCbl, 5c, 9 both. Jupiter Images: 21br, 22. Bernhard Lang/Getty Images: 11tl. Remarkable (Pencils) Ltd.: 17b.
Shutterstock: OFCbr, OFCtr, 1, 6, 6–7t, 8, 10–11b, 11c, 11br, 12–13 both, 14, 15b, 16t, 17t, 18–19 all, 20l, OBC.
Mark Edward Smith/photolibrary.com: 15t. Hayley Terry: OFCtl and throughout. Ingrid Visser/Splashdown Direct/
Rex Features: 7b. David Woodfall/Getty Images: 4–5c

Every effort has been made to trace copyright holders, and we apologize in advance for any omissions.
We would be pleased to insert the appropriate acknowledgments in any subsequent edition of this publication.

Contents

What is recycling?

When something is thrown away, the materials it is made of can be used to make something else. This is called recycling.

paper recycling bin

How much do we throw away?

Most families throw away between one and two tons of garbage each year—which is around the weight of an elephant! Industries also produce a lot of **waste**.

What can be recycled?

Many materials can be recycled, including paper, cardboard, metal, plastic, and glass. A lot of things are made of more than one material. These must be taken apart and sorted into their different materials before they are recycled.

Where does recycling start?

The first stage in recycling is separating garbage into different materials. You can help do this at home or at school by using recycling bins.

home recycling bin

How are things sorted?

When your garbage reaches a recycling plant, someone sorts it into different types. There are also machines that can help sort things.

5

Why recycle?

When people make new things by recycling old ones, it saves energy, uses up less material, and causes less **pollution**.

How does recycling reduce pollution?

A lot of garbage is buried under the ground at landfills. As this garbage rots away, it can produce dangerous substances. Underground water sometimes spreads these substances, causing pollution.

landfill

Does recycling save energy?

Often it does. It takes 20 times as much energy to produce **aluminum** from underground sources as it does to recycle it.

Why is it good to use less materials?

The materials we use come from many sources. For example, plastic comes from oil and metal comes from the ground. When we have used up all of these things, they will be gone forever.

Mature forests take many hundreds of years to grow. Recycling paper means fewer trees need to be cut down.

How does recycling help the climate?

Garbage is often burned, and when it is, **greenhouse gases** are produced. These greenhouse gases make the world hotter, which causes problems for many people and animals, such as these polar bears in the **Arctic**.

Talking Point

How does the climate affect polar bears?

Polars bears live in the icy parts of the Arctic and hunt their food on the ice. As our planet warms up, the ice is melting, so the bears have nowhere to hunt the seals they eat.

polar bears

WORD WIZARD!
energy
the thing that is needed to make or do anything. Electricity and heat are both types of energy.

What are the 3 Rs?

The 3 Rs of waste management are reduce, reuse, and recycle. They are all ways to make better use of materials.

How can we reduce the materials we use?

There are many ways to do this. For example, **documents** can be read on a computer instead of printing them out. This reduces the amount of paper that is used.

What can we reuse?

Among many other things, clothes, shoes, and eyeglasses can be reused by other people. One easy way to make sure things are reused is to take them to a thrift store.

computer

bin for recycling plastic

bin for recycling glass

bin for recycling paper

Who are the 3 Rs for?

Everyone! We can all reduce and reuse things, and we can all help recycle materials, too.

You can buy secondhand clothes at a thrift store.

WORD WIZARD!
secondhand
used by someone else

Recycling paper

People use an enormous amount of paper. Making recycled paper uses less than one half of the energy and water that making new paper does.

Can all types of paper be recycled?

Yes, but some types are very expensive to recycle, so it is not worth doing. Glossy paper is especially expensive to recycle. This is because the materials that make it glossy have to be taken out first.

How is paper recycled?

First it is chopped up and mixed with water to make pulp. Then the pulp is squeezed and dried.

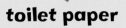

toilet paper

What is recycled paper used for?

All sorts of things. Toilet paper, shopping bags, notebook paper, envelopes—even home **insulation** and cat litter can be made from recycled paper.

Talking Point

How much paper do we throw away?

In most homes, around one fifth of garbage is paper. Most of this can be recycled—it just needs to be sorted out! Check with an adult before sorting your garbage.

How are metals recycled?

Almost all metals are found as **ores**, which are types of rocks. Digging ores out of the ground, and removing metals from them, takes a lot of energy.

Which metals are recycled?

The two metals that are most worthwhile to recycle are **steel** and aluminum. Steel is used for all sorts of machines and buildings. Aluminum is often used to make vehicles and also for making cans and foil.

aluminum cans

WORD WIZARD!

molten

describes something that is melted so much that it becomes a liquid

How are metals recycled?

Metal objects are broken up, crushed, and melted. The molten metal can then be used to make new objects.

molten steel

Talking Point

Are recycled metals as good as metals that come from ores?

Yes. They are just as good, because they have exactly the same properties, such as strength, weight, and color.

magnet

How can metals be separated?

Steel can be easily separated from other materials by using a **magnet** to pull it away. Most other materials are not pulled away by the magnet, so they are left behind.

13

Recycling plastic and glass

Around one fourth of the garbage that is buried under the ground is plastic. Unfortunately, it can be difficult to recycle. Glass, on the other hand, is easy to recycle.

plastic toys

Why are plastics difficult to recycle?

Different plastics are often used together—many bottles have a body made of one type of plastic and a lid made of another type. These have to be separated by hand. Even after they have been separated, plastics cannot simply be melted like metals or pulped like paper.

How is glass recycled?

Just like metal, glass can be melted and then used to make new things.

molten glass

Walkway paved with glassphalt at Honolulu Zoo in Hawaii

What is recycled glass used for?

Recycled glass is often used to make bottles, or it can be turned into glassphalt, a material that is used to make roads and sidewalks.

Talking Point

What is biodegradable plastic?

Most plastics are made from things that don't rot away. But some plastic is made from materials that can be broken down in soil. This is called biodegradable plastic.

How are bottles sorted?

Bottles can be thrown away into bottle banks that have separate containers for clear, brown, and green glass.

Concrete and tires

A large amount of concrete is used to make buildings and roads, and making it produces a great deal of greenhouse gas and uses a lot of water.

What is concrete?

Concrete is a very hard and strong material used in building. It is a mixture of **cement**, **gravel**, sand, and water.

cement mixer

How is concrete recycled?

Concrete is crushed in a special machine. The pieces are often used to make new concrete.

concrete crusher

How are recycled tires used?

Tires can be shredded and used to make all sorts of things, including drainpipes, basketball courts, book covers, and doormats.

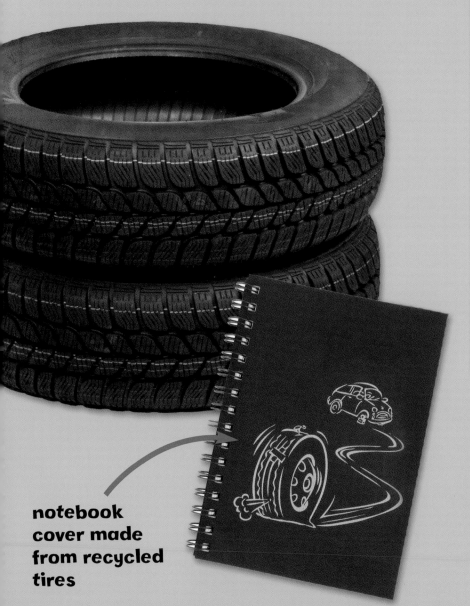

notebook cover made from recycled tires

Talking Point

Can new tires be made from recycling the rubber from old tires?

No, the rubber from old tires cannot be melted down to make new ones. Some old, worn-down tires can be repaired and used again, but many are shredded and used to make other things.

WORD WIZARD!
shredded
torn into small pieces

Around the house

We are surrounded by all kinds of equipment, and we often like to replace it—we buy new cell phones, computers, and printers. But what happens to the old ones?

Cell phones

There are millions of cell phones all over the world that are no longer used. If they are given to charities, they can be passed on to people who need them.

cell phones

Computers

Unwanted computers can also be given to other people. This does not just help the people—computers contain substances that can cause pollution if they are thrown away to be burned or buried.

Printer cartridges

Cartridges are difficult to recycle because they are made of different materials. But many can be refilled with ink and reused many times.

Batteries

Batteries contain **harmful** substances, so throwing them away can cause problems. Instead, we can buy rechargeable batteries that can be used over and over again.

Talking point

What should you do before giving a computer to someone else?

Make sure you have copied all of your files from the computer. Then reformat the hard drive. This helps make sure no one can see your old files. They might have private information in them that you wouldn't want anyone else to read.

flashlight

rechargeable batteries

19

Composting

It is not only things made by people that can be recycled. Leftover food and garden trash can be recycled, too, by turning it into compost.

industrial composter

What is compost?

Compost is the remains of food and garden waste that has rotted. Earthworms help break it down. It is used to grow new plants.

Making compost

Industrial composters turn huge amounts of waste into compost. They make sure the temperature and dampness are just right for the waste to rot.

Talking Point

What type of kitchen waste can be composted?

Only raw fruit and vegetable peels and scraps should be composted. It is possible to compost meat, fish, and cooked foods, but adding them to your composter might attract rats and make it smell bad.

Is compost easy to make?

It is if you have a garden. You just need to put vegetable peels and garden waste into a special container called a composter, and it will slowly turn into compost.

What can I do with old toys?

Most toys are made of several materials, so they are not easy to recycle. But, unless they are broken, old toys are very easy to reuse.

a market for secondhand items

recycled toys

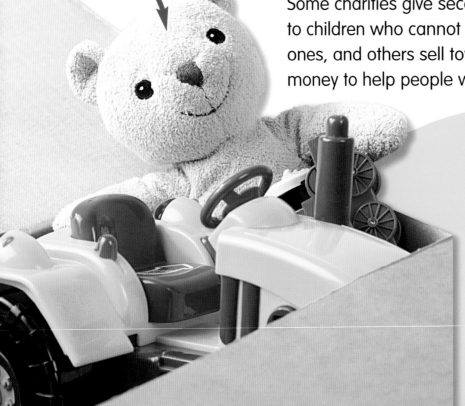

How are toys reused?

Some charities give secondhand toys to children who cannot afford new ones, and others sell toys and use the money to help people who need it.

What else can be reused?

Clothes, shoes, and books can all be reused in the same way as toys.

Where can I buy secondhand things?

You can buy them in many places. Thrift stores are a good place to start, but they can also be bought online or at yard sales and flea markets. Some very old secondhand things are called vintage.

Can thrift stores sell all kinds of things?

Thrift stores can sell most things. They can't sell things that run on electricity unless they have someone to test them, because they might not be safe.

It's usually cheaper to buy books at secondhand bookstores or markets like this one.

Talking Point

What are antiques?

Antiques are very old things that some people like to collect. Antique furniture, jewelry, and books can be worth a lot of money because they are difficult to find.

23

Glossary

aluminum a very light metal

Arctic the region around the North Pole. A lot of it is frozen ocean.

battery a thing that stores electricity. Batteries are sometimes used to power machines.

cement a mixture of limestone and clay

document something containing information. Letters and many computer files are called documents.

gravel small stones mixed with sand

greenhouse gas a gas in the air that traps the Sun's heat

harmful bad for people or other living things

insulation materials that are used to reduce the amount of heat, noise, or electricity that moves from one place to another

magnet something that attracts some types of metal, including iron

ore a type of rock that contains a useful substance

pollution things that can damage the health of living things

steel a strong metal

waste things that are thrown away

Index